# WOK

## TREE
## HERITAGE
## RAMBLES

# MARTIN HUMPHREY

## PHOTOGRAPHS   DARREN HEMSLEY

PUBLISHED
Chris Howkins,
70, Grange Road,
New Haw,
WEYBRIDGE,
Surrey, KT15 3RH.

PRINTED
Unwin Brothers Limited,
The Gresham Press,
OLD WOKING,
Surrey, England.
GU22 9LH.

# CONTENTS

# FOREWORD

As Chairman of the Surrey branch of The Men of the Trees, the International Society for the Planting and Protection of Trees, I have encouraged the campaign for the continuence of planting a wide range of trees.

Through a newspaper report of one of our planting schemes I met Chris Howkins and it was through his support for this campaign that we have produced jointly this addition to his series of heritage rambles books.

I am grateful to my wife Cecilia for her patience during the research and writing of this book and to my sons Mark and Duncan for their invaluable help in word processing. My thanks also to Darren Hemsley for his photographic services.

MAPS - Although these have been created with care they are nevertheless only sketch maps. They are simplified and not drawn to scale.

## IMPORTANT

The trees in this book can be viewed from the public highway but in so doing please take care not to invade people's privacy and not to enter private property or steal twigs etc. off other people's plants.

# INTRODUCTION

There is nowhere else in the country quite like Woking - for its trees. Only about 35 different trees returned to Britain after the last Ice Age, some 12,000 years ago. Man, however, has introduced well over 1500 more and a very large percentage of those can be seen around Woking.

Many of these introductions were first propagated from the Woking nurseries, from the late 18th century through the 19th century. Many of the new hybrids and selected strains were developed first of all at the same Woking nurseries, making them of foremost importance in the horticultural world. Today, most of the nursery fields have been built over but survivors of the nursery stock still grow as fine mature specimens in the local streets and gardens. They are, therefore, some of the oldest of their kind in the country.

They will not last for ever and the need for replacements must be born in mind. The storms of October 1987 and January 1990, the droughts of 1989 and 1990, have all impressed this upon us. They have also made significant changes to our landscape and the text has been ammended accordingly.

The text is presented as four easy rambles, selected to encompass a wide range of trees that can be admired from the public highway. Hopefully more people will realise that each tree has its own history, which can add immeasurably to our appreciation of them. Some indication of this is given in the text. Obviously there is only room to highlight a few of the trees out of the hundreds that can be seen on these rambles and so an identification handbook would be useful to take with you. Of the many excellent books in print those by Alan Mitchell are recommended, such as "The Trees of Britain and Europe" published by Collins. For the story of the Woking nurseries see E.J.Willson's "Nurserymen to the World".

# WYCH HILL

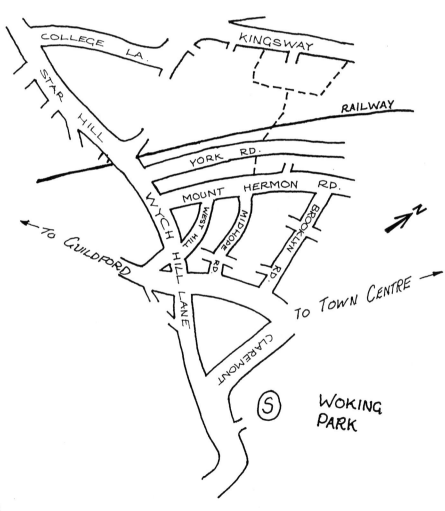

# RAMBLE AREA 1.

## WYCH HILL - STAR HILL - MOUNT HERMON

**STARTING AT WOKING PARK** - Most of the land on this south side of the railway was farmland until the 1880s and those rural times are recorded in such names as Turnoak Lane, Orchard Mains and Wych Hill, named after Wych Elms. This tree only reproduces by seed and so it is now infrequently seen, following Dutch Elm Disease, whereas the English Elm spreads by suckers and has thus been rapidly re-establishing itself.

The area around Woking Park was developed after 1883 when Cross Lanes Farm was sold for 'superior character housing.' The farm had covered 136 acres from the Guildford Road eastwards to White Rose Lane and north to Heathside Road. Part of it was saved as the Constitution Hill Recreation Ground, renamed Woking Park in 1927.

In 1910 a double avenue of trees was planted behind the swimming pool and about half of these still survive. Measurement show that they have been increasing in girth at about one inch (2.5cm) per year - a useful guide to the rate of tree growth in the Woking area.

## MOVE DOWN TO ENTRANCE FROM KINGFIELD ROAD

Alterations to the Park in 1932 included the current access road complete with concrete bridge over the Hoe Stream. The accompanying treescape has matured to give a rich variety of evergreens and deciduous trees, conifers and broadleaved trees, enhancing the area throughout the year. Of particular interest are two Dawn Redwoods(Metasequoia glyptostoboides), planted in about 1960, one either side of the entrance. According to fossil evidence whole forests of this tree were inhabited by Pterodactyls and Brontosaurs during the Jurassic Period but then the tree disappears from the fossil record some 20 million years ago. In 1941 a large specimen was found in Central China and seeds were first brought to Britain in 1948.

## TURN RIGHT AS YOU LEAVE THE PARK

In this rich treescape notice the London Planes bordering Kingfield Road. They are the most popular street trees in the world as they can survive urban conditions and drought. They are hybrids between the Oriental Plane and the American Plane, first occuring in the mid 17thC. when the two parent trees were growing together in the Lambeth garden of the royal gardener John Tradescant. At least, that's the most popular explanation but not all botanists agree on the origins or even the parents.

**ELM BRIDGE** is one of the few old 'elm' names in the County and before 1891/2 was made of wood, hence the earlier name Ell Bridge which meant plank bridge. Elm timber is very water resistant and indeed was bored to make water pipes and well pumps. Despite being called English Elm it comes from Southern Europe and was introduced probably in pre-Roman times.

Around this area can be seen dense hedges of English Elm regenerating from the rootstocks after Dutch Elm Disease. The epidemic between 1920 and 1945 arose from the importation of unbarked logs from America, resulting in the loss of some 10% of Elms in Southern England. Thus imports of unbarked logs were prohibited but relaxed in 1949. By the late 1960s a new aggressive strain had arrived from Canada, killing some 15 million trees in Britain and now spreading across Europe. It is so called because the Dutch have studied it to breed new disease resistant strains of the tree.

## CONTINUE UP WYCH HILL LANE

The avenue of trees with deeply rugged bark are False Acacias which were introduced from North America via France. They belong to the genus Robinia, named after Jean Robin, botanist to the King of France, Henry IV. It is a valuable tree to plant because its flowers are much favoured by bees.

LEFT - The 'fossil' tree, the Dawn Redwood, gives a strong accent to the variety of tree forms in the rich treescape at the entrance to Woking Park.

## TURNOAK ROUNDABOUT

Designed as a 'traffic circus' in 1934, it was Woking's first roundabout. Alterations in 1985 brought the carriageway so close to one of the English Oaks on the island that it is now dying back.

Part of the 1934 work involved diverting Guildford Road, leaving the old section as Guildford Lane. Several fine trees were saved which were originally on part of Jackman's Nursery. Thus near the junction with Guildford Lane is a spreading maple with silvery backs to its small lobed leaves. This is Acer saccharinium from S.E.Canada down to Louisiana, introduced in 1725 and from which maple syrup can be made. It is not the same Acer as the one in commercial use for syrup.

Look down the grass towards Guildford, as in the photograph below, and you are looking down through the Jackman heritage. The tall upright tree to the right is a Dawyck Beech - the column-shaped version of the Common Beech, found in Peebles, Scotland, about 1860 and not generally planted until 1927. Here it fits the scene aesthetically, between the False Acacias on the left and the Silver Birch on the right.

The photograph above was taken closer to the Dawyck Beech to show the beautiful spreading Indian Bean Tree in the foreground. Apart from helping to close the view and break the lines of vertical trunks this tree adds beauty of its own for this is the yellow-leaved form which lightens the heavy greens of summer and at that time the tree becomes covered with great panicles of white flowers.

## WALK ON UP WYCH HILL LANE

This ramble leaves the former Jackman nursery fields behind but the Jackman heritage is highlighted again in Ramble No.2. Continuing through the present tree-scape, turn left for a diversion into Wych Hill Waye and look for the Common Walnut on the left.

Walnuts were probably first introduced by the Romans for their nuts but in time it was the timber that became highly prized. Surrey was formerly the premier county for its production. Although its use for furniture making may come to mind it was first choice for making rifle butts and this caused the felling of the Surrey groves, first for the American War of Independence and then for the Napoleonic Wars.

On the right is one of over 200 variants of the
Lawson Cypress, some of which have been raised in the
County at Ottershaw, Grayswood, etc.  In the centre of
the road is a huge Atlas Cedar, introduced from the
Atlas Mountains of Algeria and Morocco in 1845, where
both this, and the blue form, are indigenous.

The photograph above shows the one tree you cannot miss
in Wych Hill Waye. Islanded in the road is this huge
Atlas Cedar, first introduced to this country in 1845
from the Atlas Mountains of Algeria and Morocco.  There
the tree is a native, together with the blue form.
The great spreading boughs, right over the road, are a
delight to pass under and its overall stature seems to
reduce everything else in scale, helping to keep the
close inviting.

LEAVE THE CLOSE AND TURN LEFT TO CONTINUE UP
WYCH HILL LANE

At the junction with Mount Hermon Road there is a line of Common Limes, known in America as Basswoods, and gardeners may remember tying plants with lengths of 'bass' stripped from the inner bark of this tree. The timber is valuable too, especially for carving, of which Grinling Gibbons was the greatest master. Today they are valued for the rich nectar in their sweetly scented flowers which is important for feeding bees.

Continue up the hill, noting the mature English Oaks and Beeches which indicate the age of this route. Cross over the railway bridge and look ahead to the dense canopy of trees in the grounds of 'Birbank'. The tallest is a Wellingtonia, the largest plant on Earth. To the right is a group of Douglas Firs, also renowned for height and for structural quality timber. Dark Yews add to the evergreen quality of this planting, enlivened seasonally by more bright green Robinias.

The provision of the roundabout in 1983 to serve Wych Hill Park necessitated felling a huge Deodar Cedar and this was promptly replaced with a new sapling to perpetuate Woking's rich heritage. The planting of this 'exotic' has been balanced by 'natives' with a group of five Wild Cherries (Prunus avium) to enhance the landscaping by the small service road of the roundabout.

At Orchard Mains, notice a fine mixed group of two Black Poplars, two Deodar Cedars, a Wellingtonia, a Copper Beech and a Common Lime.

## TURN RIGHT ALONG COLLEGE LANE

This area of large forest trees is dwindling. Still surviving are some fine Sweet Chestnuts, Scots Pines, and on the left, in the garden of 'St.Catherine's' two tall Wellingtonias.

AT THE END TURN LEFT AND WALK UNDER RAILWAY BRIDGE. CROSS THE ROAD TO SKIRT ROUND THE RIGHT HAND SIDE OF THE ROUNDABOUT AHEAD, READY TO TURN RIGHT INTO KINGSWAY, BUT, PAUSE AT THE ROUNDABOUT TO LOOK BACK OVER IT TO THE TREES BEYOND.

The impressive group of trees, backed by the wooded
hillside rising behind the housing up to St.Johns, is
marking an important site. This was part of Goldsworth
Nursery, one of several that rose to make Woking of
world importance in horticulture. It was founded in
1760 by James Turner and then sold to Robert Donald in
the early 1800s. By the 1850s and 60s it was in decline
and had dwindled to 24 acres. Not for long. In 1877
it was bought by Walter Slocock who so revived it that
by the time of his death in 1929 it extended for 420
acres with 161 employees.

The view, as can be seen from this photograph, is well
and truly dominated by the two Wellingtonias, creating
an interesting skyscape with their bold silhouettes.
Beneath them, to the left, are the great spreading boughs
of a Cedar of Lebanon. In contrast, notice the elegant
spire of the bright green Dawn Redwood.

This whole collection is worth a good look and from a variety of directions. It was supplemented in 1990 by the new planting of trees and shrubs on the roundabout. Included were three Liquidamber Trees, famed for their autumn colours, which will look increasingly grand here as the trees mature against the dark background.

## RIGHT INTO KINGSWAY AND RIGHT AT DELARA WAY. AT FIRST HOUSE TURN LEFT ONTO PATHWAY AND IMMEDIATELY RIGHT

This path through to York Road takes you past a strip of land wide enough for Oak trees. These provide a good screen to the extensive railway sidings below and illustrate the value of including large forest trees, in suitable places, within the urban area. Before the first bridge on the right is the blue foliage of the Eucalyptus - the world's fastest growing tree and its tallest broadleaf tree.

## CROSS OVER YORK ROAD TO CONTINUE ON PATH. TURN LEFT AT MOUNT HERMON ROAD.

Near the back of the path by Mount Hermon Close there is a good example of Robinia with delicate compound leaves contrasting with the large lobed leaves of the Red Oak beyond. The subtleties continue with, a little further on, an English Oak on the right contrasting with the lighter Ash-leaved Maple outside 'Stoneleigh'. Before turning into Brooklyn Road notice the Red Horse Chestnut, Sequoia and Deodar outside 'Lampeter House'. A little further on look for an Oriental Plane outside 'Leeward'. This species is believed to be one of the parents of the London Plane noted earlier by Woking Park. The Oriental Plane can be distinguished from the London Plane by the more deeply lobed leaves with wavy outlines.

## TURN INTO BROOKLYN ROAD

Look for the Weeping Beech at Brooklyn Court on the right. This cultivar, one of the Jackman introductions, is created by grafting the 'Pendula' strain onto a rootstock of the normal Beech, Fagus sylvatica. Here the graft is clearly visible about 2m up the trunk.

Looking down 'Belgrave Manor' notice the two closely
planted pines - a Scots Pine with its distinctive rich
orange bark contrasting with a dark Corsican Pine. They
give scale to the surrounding buildings while allowing
gardens to be developed underneath them as it is quite
natural for them to lose their lower branches. It is
tragic that the character of the Woking area, favoured
originally for its beautiful pines on the heath, is now
being allowed to gradually change simply because it is
unfashionable to plant conifers.

TURN RIGHT INTO GUILDFORD ROAD and note the tall
Douglas Fir at Greenfield School, together with a Yew
and, giving seasonal variety, a new flush of English
Elm.

## TURN RIGHT INTO MIDHOPE ROAD

On the right is an Ash-leaved Maple and a line of
pollarded Common Limes while over on the boundary of
Corner House and Ellingham is another large English
Walnut. The nameboard for 'Ellingham' is set in a
wall to retain the unexpected Canary Palm, Phoenix
canariensis, saved from the original garden. Alas the
unimaginative new plantings of Silver Birch and Whitebeam will make no significant replacement for the
gradual loss of forest trees. We need to plant now
for the eventual renewal of such trees as the Douglas
Fir opposite No.38, the Horse Chestnut opposite No.30,
the Ash at Midhope Gardens, the Corsican Pine by No.12
and the Common Lime opposite, if the unique leafy
character of this area is to be perpetuated.

## TURN LEFT INTO MOUNT HERMON ROAD

Many gardens in this area have Magnolias which are well
worth coming to see in full bloom in early spring. Also
there are many Japanese Maples, like the handsome one at
No.29A. On a larger scale there is a huge Copper Beech
at 'Hendersyde' with a Western Red Cedar opposite. It
is this mixture of tall forest trees and smaller gardenworthy trees and shrubs that makes for such a beautiful
and worthwhile environment, as illustrated in the next
photograph.

## TURN LEFT INTO WEST HILL ROAD

At the junction you might like to cross over to the church for the view captured by the photographer for the scene reproduced below. Here a 'country lane' atmosphere has developed with mature trees dappling the road with their shadows and a rich variety of trees and shrubs in the gardens to screen the houses. How bleak it must have been when the houses were new.

The three conifers on the right are Corsican Pines and the deciduous broadleaf on the left is a Horse Chestnut.

As the road bends there is a huge Red Oak in the garden of 'Tettenhall' which gives one of several opportunities near town centre to be able to stand and stare right up into the great spreading boughs of a forest tree. This one was probably planted soon after the house was built in 1905 - judging from its girth of some 130 inches or nearly 4.5 metres.

At 'Westlands' there is a variegated Ashleaf Maple
which has become very popular in recent years and with
it another increasingly popular tree, the yellow-leaved
Honey Locust, Gleditsia tricanthos 'Sunburst'. Of an
older tradition is the red Horse Chestnut by the gate
of 'Beech House' on the right.

Opposite is the close-clipped Yew topiary illustrated
below. It makes an unusual and interesting addition
to Woking's tree heritage. Its robust rounded shapes
work beautifully against the straight linear qualities
of the house architecture. Topiary was introduced
probably by the Romans and became fashionable again
in Tudor times.

Finally, at the bottom of the road, stands a Silver
Pendant Lime, Tilia petiolaris, of uncertain origin.
Some think it is a variant of the Silver Lime while
others argue for an origin in the Caucasus. It is only
propagated by grafting onto a Broad-leaved Lime and is
particularly gardenworthy for being free of greenfly.

TURN LEFT TO RETURN TO THE STARTING POINT

There are hundreds of different trees around Woking
and each has its own 'biography' which adds a whole
new dimension to any appreciation of the tree heritage.
Some have been in the service of man for hundreds of
years, providing not just timber but a wide variety
of other raw materials, such as the bass and cork
highlighted in the text. Others have become the centre
of superstition and folklore; the Vikings believed all
men were descended from Ash trees and women from Elms.
Then there are the stories of the tree's discovery and
introduction and an example of one of these is outlined
below.

# WELLINGTONIAS

Many people comment on those trees in America that are
so massive that tunnels have been driven through them,
large enough for American cars to drive through. Few
people, however, realise that this same tree is well
represented in Woking - the Wellingtonia.

The tale of its discovery takes us to the Californian
Goldrush of the 1850s and to a camp of the Union Water
Company. From there a local hunter named A.T.Dowd set
out one day to shoot game and succeeded in wounding a
grizzly bear. In trying to track it through the forest
he discovered the largest tree he'd ever seen but no
one back at camp was interested. However, the next
Sunday Dowd roused the camp saying he'd shot the largest
grizzly bear he'd ever seen and needed help to bring it
back. There was no shortage of volunteers.

Leading them to his tree Dowd pointed it out as the
largest grizzly he'd ever seen. The others were
amazed by his discovery and helped him explore further
to find the Calaveras Grove of Sierra Redwoods, as
they are called in America. To the Mono Indian tribe
in the Sierra Nevada mountains it was known as Woh-Woh-
Nau ofter the call of the owl whose spirit was believed
to protect the tree. It was no use against the foresters
who began felling them. One, nicknamed 'Mark Twain',
stood 101m high until sliced up in 1891 and it is one
of those slices that can be seen in London's Natural
History Museum today.

The largest survivor today is 'The General Sherman Tree' in the Sequoia National Park with an estimated weight of timber above ground of 5,300 tons plus another 300 tons of root. Its height is 83m, its basal girth 30.8m, with the lowest branch 40m from the ground and 2.1m diameter. It is probably some 2,500 years old.

The story does not end there. With the introduction of the tree into Britain came trans-Atlantic wrangles as to what it should be called; wrangles that lasted until 1938! That tale is outlined on page 33.

The largest local specimen of the Wellingtonia is at the bottom of St.Johns Hill.

Other fascinating tales come from the biographies of the plant collectors would risked life and limb, literally, to explore uncharted regions of the world in a search for valuable new plants - raw materials for Britain's expanding industrialism, food plants for Britain's increasing population, rare status plants for the great gardens, and so on. Outlined below is the life of one of the greatest of these explorers.

# DAVID DOUGLAS

David Douglas (1799-1834) was the son of a Scottish stonemason and was three when he started school. By the age of eleven, when he left school, he was so good at botany that he became an apprentice at the Scone Botanic Garden. At twenty he obtained a place at the Glasgow Botanic Garden and in 1823 was engaged at the Horticultural Society's London Garden. After only three months he was appointed their first 'plant scout' to go abroad to collect specimens.

His first trip, to the Eastern coast of America, was very successful and he arrived back in London loaded with specimens and boxes of seeds.

His second trip, six months later, was to the Pacific coast. The voyage, in a sailing ship round Cape Horn, lasted 256 days and brought them to Fort Vancouver on the north bank of the Columbia River. This was the main trading post of the Hudson Bay Company. From there, despite the impossibly difficult wet and cold conditions he collected over 500 different plants in six months, including the fir that is named after him. These he dispatched in the 'Dyrad' but such was his care as a scientist he also sent 197 boxes of seed to the East coast by an overland route in case the 'Dyrad' was shipwrecked. Both consignments arrived safely.

Over the next two years he travelled extensively through the Pacific coast mainland - 2,400 miles on foot and by boat over the most difficult wilderness. He reached the Arctic port of York Factory, right across the continent on the Atlantic seaboard, in September 1827. October found him back in Portsmouth laden with huge quantities of seed and samples - more than any botanist had ever brought back to England before.

His final expedition was to the Pacific north west in 1830. There followed a year of terrific toil and physical hardship, including being overturned from his canoe into icy waters, days of near starvation, danger from hostile Indians, failing eyesight, failing strength.

Needing a respite, he sailed to Honolulu. Here, while walking in the mountains, he fell into a pit concealed with grass to trap wild animals. Unfortunately he was not the first victim and was gored to death by an enraged bull.

Today, an impressive granite memorial to this pioneer botanist stands in the churchyard of Old Scone. On it are carved some of the many species of trees and plants that he introduced to this country.

# ST JOHNS

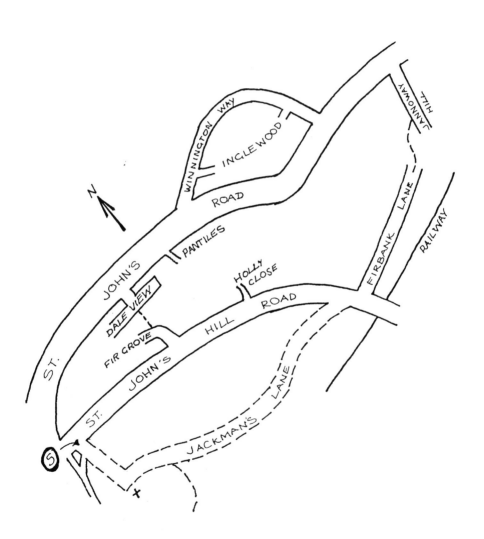

RAMBLE AREA 2

ST JOHNS

STARTING IN CHURCH ROAD AT ITS JUNCTION WITH
ST JOHNS HILL ROAD

This route passes from the early development of St.Johns
through the features of the great nursery age to the
most recent developments in Goldsworth Park.

Here in Church Road it is easier to picture the earlier
days as you note four grand oaks that make such an
architectural feature at the entrance to the lower
trackway.  The land climbs steadily, past a particularly
old oak in the left bank which was well grown even
before the builders arrived.  At the top is the church,
begun in 1840 and one of the earliest by a man who
later became outstanding - Sir George Gilbert Scott.

His building sits among trees and has a particularly
effective backing of mixed deciduous and evergreen
trees.  The front is set off by an attractive sloping
and hedged burial ground.

ABOVE - Looking from St.John's Church down over the
slope to the old Oak trees.  Parts of this landscape
are older than the church and its associated development.

25

Prominent, front left of the church, is an impressive
example of the Weeping Beech, Fagus sylvatica 'Pendula'.
This is a Woking speciality as it was the Knaphill
Nursery which first introduced this and the Fern-leafed
Beech into Britain from Germany in 1826. Even today
there is only a handful of Weeping Beech in the area
and no Fern-leafed Beech of any size that I have yet
located, other than the original which can still be
found at Knaphill Nursery. A leaflet giving details of
all their trees is available from the checkout.

In Alan Mitchell's description of Knaphill Nursery he
states that their Weeping Beech, planted to the east of
the spine road, has become so spectacular and extra-
ordinary that it defies adequate description.

Before setting off on the ramble it is useful perhaps
to outline the story of Jackmans' world-famous
nursery which will feature en route.

William Jackman (1763-1840) from a family of gardeners
is thought to have founded the nursery at St.Johns.
He built up a thriving business, finding that the
light acid sandy soil was ideal for raising cuttings.
He started with 50 acres, known as the Home Portion

and home was 'The Hollies', a large house between
Jackmans Lane and St.Johns Hill Road, which is still
standing, divided into flats and renamed 'Deerstead
House'.

The business continued under William's two sons,
George (1801-69) and Henry, until the latter left the
partnership by mutual agreement in 1832. By this time
it was called 'Woking Nursery' and covered areas on
both sides of St.John's Hill Road and the Goldsworth
Road, up to Waterer's property called 'Goldsworth
Nursery'. Jackmans were now trading in a wide range of
plants, especially trees and shrubs, being particularly
successful with peach trees for the new enthusiasm for
stove houses.

In 1869 George Jackman II (1837-89) took over the
nursery on the death of his father. He was the man who
became a leader in the current enthusiasm for the
Clematis and produced many fine hybrids which are still
grown today. Some were given local names, such as
'Belle of Woking' and 'Countess of Lovelace' but the
one that became a world-wide best seller was named
Jackmanii. They have all derived from just one plant
in a batch of 300 seedlings that first flowered in
1862. In due course an improved strain was spotted
and marketed as Clematis Jackmanii Superba.

By the time George Jackman II died in 1889 the nursery
had enlarged to 300 acres but instructions in his will
led to arguments with the Trustees and 40 acres of the
nursery at St Johns had to be sold. The business was
transferred to Bedfords Farm off Egley Road which he
had bought from his brother-in-law, Mr.Lee, earlier.

Many unusual trees and shrubs were left behind at St
Johns and when the nursery site was later developed
for housing so these specimens were often retained in
the gardens where they have now matured. Some of these
valuable trees will be highlighted along the following
route.

LEFT - The Weeping Beech at St.John's churchyard
where its lower branches have been left to trail
so beautifully down over the headstones.

FROM THE CHURCH FOLLOW JACKMANS LANE ROUND TO
THE LEFT. AT THE FORK KEEP TO THE TOP TRACK.
CONTINUE AHEAD EVEN WHEN THE TRACK BECOMES A
FOOTPATH.

Opposite the church car park, on the bank of 'West End'
you get a good close view of a mature Coast Redwood,
Sequoia sempervirens although it lost its top in the
1987 gale. The tree was first introduced into Britain
in 1843 and gets its specific name, sempervirens, which
means ever-living, from the fact that this is one of
the very few conifers that will sprout from the stump
if the tree is cut down.

Following the track through the woods there's a peep
over the first gate on the left to see three of the
Jackman heritage trees. In the centre of the view
there's a magnificent specimen, with perfect pyramidal
form, of the yellow Lawson's Cypress, Chamaecyparis
Lawsoniana 'Lutea' which is just one of a very extensive
range of cultivars of this tree, from all shades of
green through to yellow and almost blue. With so much
variety in both colour and form it has become one of
our most abundant trees. Its thick foliage is very
valuable to small birds which can shelter in it from
winter cold.

Behind the Cypress are the pale green leaves of a
Tulip Tree which is one of several fine specimens in
the gardens of the St Johns Hill Road district. In
this country they only flower eratically but the ones
in this district flower every year without exception.
Look in June for the yellow flowers (like lily-flowered
tulips) among the leaves and enjoy the tree again in
autumn when the foliage turns an attractive gold.

In winter, when the leaves are off the Tulip Tree, is
the best time to see the third special tree which is
growing behind it - a Wellingtonia or Giant Sequoia.
It has been placed in the genus Sequoiadendron to
distinguish it from the Coast Redwood Sequoia noted
above. The name commemorates Sequoyah, a Cherokee
Indian leader.

Where the track becomes a path there is a Douglas Fir
in the garden on the left. Although it has no top it
is still worth a look for anyone learning how to
recognise the tree because it shows clearly one of its
important features - the way the bark on the lower trunk
turns a dark rich brown with deep fissures.

## CONTINUE ALONG THE PATH THROUGH THE WOODS

Gorse bushes show this was once heathland but they have
been overtopped by invading birch and now the Birches
are being crowded out by Oaks. It is a good example of
the natural regeneration of woodland. Now that the oaks
are reaching dominance so the typical oakwood under-
growth is developing, with Holly and Brambles etc.
The Sycamore, a notorious coloniser, is present too
but so are unexpected species like the Spindle.

## ON REACHING THE ROADWAY CONTINUE AHEAD

Now the landscape becomes close with housing and small
gardens, very rich in trees and shrubs, but difficult
to view without risking invasion of people's privacy.

That said, there is a striking Purple Maple on the left
boundary that is large enough to enjoy as you approach.
It is now mature enough to show off its strong branching
pattern and distinctive bark. Almost immediately after
it is a tree that looks like a Horse Chestnut but come
in the spring and you'll find yellow flowers instead
of the familiar white. This is the Horse Chestnut's
American relation, the Yellow Buckeye, Aesculus flava,
from the Appalachien Mountains. Come in the autumn
and you'll find the foliage turns a clear gold.

On the right at 'Kelwood' lived William Jackman and his
family. The outbuildings survive on either side too,
having been converted into bungalows in 1953. That
on the left was the pay office while the bellshed
still has its rooftop campanile from which a bell was
rung to summon the workers from the nursery fields.

More grand trees appear on the left and these can be
seen well from St.Johns Hill Road so...

## TURN LEFT INTO ST JOHNS HILL ROAD

Within a few yards of turning left along St Johns Hill
Road there are good views (from the pavement on the
right hand side) of a Swamp Cypress, Taxodium distichum,
in the garden on the left. Even though it stands among
other heritage trees it can be easily identified by its
bright green summer foliage, Being a deciduous conifer
it is bare in winter, hence its American name of Bald
Cypress. In autumn it turns a beautiful bronze and will
often keep its foliage up to Christmas. It is called a
Swamp Cypress because it loves to grow in the tidal
creeks of its homeland, from Delaware to Texas and for
1,000 miles up the Mississipi. In these places it
grows curious woody protuberances from its spreading
roots. These 'knees' can grow eight feet high but,
being hollow, are only a few inches thick. Their exact
purpose is not known but they are thought to help the
roots to breathe. Despite growing naturally in water-
logged conditions they will grow in most soils and even
survive drought conditions; it's certainly very dry up
here. It is also very exposed but the tree has adapted
to withstand hurricanes; in the 1987 Great Storm this
tree stood firm, although the top was damaged.

A few yards further on look for the impressive facade
of 'Deerstead House', the aforementioned headquarters
of the Jackman business.

TURN RIGHT INTO FIRGROVE

Glance over your left shoulder and you'll see another
fine group of trees: a Coast Redwood on the left, a
Giant Sequoia on its own and then on the far right the
unmistakeable column of an Incense Cedar.

KEEPING TO THE FOOTPATH ON THE RIGHT pause on
the brow for a wide view over Woking town centre, seen
islanded in the trees to give the impression of a
'country town'. From here the softening, masking value
of including forest trees in suitable places within
the urban area is well demonstrated. The prime example
is the way the massive B.A.T. building appears so much
smaller when the Giant Sequoia to its left appears to
be nearly as tall (it's in the front garden of
'Inglewood' on Goldsworth Park). To the left again

the distinctive branching pattern of a Cedar plays its part and yet for another contrast, to the left again, a magnificent Corsican Pine fits between the houses. This view could so easily be a sea of rooftops had not some of the mature trees been retained. (Illustrated below)

CONTINUE DOWN THE FOOTPATH
(not recommended for wheelchairs)
The footpath is lined either side with a mixture of the Small-leaved Lime and the Broad-leaved - a good chance to compare the two.

TURN RIGHT AT ST JOHNS ROAD AND RIGHT AGAIN INTO PANTILES

Walk to the top and turn to the right to see the large and scarce Hungarian Oak, Quercus frainetto, outside No.16. How different are these large deeply cut leaves compared with those of the English Oak. The lean of this tree, incidently, is due to the 1990 gale rather than being a natural tendency.

RETURN TO ST JOHNS ROAD AND TURN RIGHT

On the way, the massive conifer ahead of you is a
Giant  Sequoia and over by the junction with Winnington
Way  Hornbeams grow out of the footway.  Many lean
at various angles and with their roots constricted
by small concrete boxes they are unlikely to be very
successful.  Given freedom they are wonderful forest
trees but they respond well to lopping so can be used
in urban areas; indeed they were once pollarded and
coppiced to provide firewood.

In the front garden of 'Apple Tree Cottage' on the
opposite side of the road is a Brewer Spruce, Picea
brewerana; its weeping branches making an unusual
feature for a conifer.

## TURN LEFT INTO WINNINGTON WAY

Pause at the junction with Inglewood to look back at
St Johns, to appreciate more fully the grandeur of the
huge conifers that dominate either side of St.Johns
Hill Road.  Standing out clearly is the Incense Cedar
outside the tower of 'Deerstead House'.

Winnington Way follows the former trackway that gave
rear access to Goldsworth Old Nursery.  The growing
fields, buildings and glasshouses were all swept away
to create Goldsworth Park: 360 acres, 4,500 houses.

## TURN RIGHT INTO INGLEWOOD

An unusual feature, left from the former nursery, stands
before you.  The road curves round a group of specimen
conifers  which was once a show-ground plot.

At the end of the first turning on the right note a young
Deodar Cedar with its steel blue colour, beautiful all
year round, especially when covered with water droplets.
Cedars are not easy to distinguish.  For the three main
species it is helpful to look at the branching pattern,
especially at the tips and remember: Ascending – Atlas,
Descending – Deodar, Level – Lebanon

## RETURN FROM THE CUL-DE-SAC AND TAKE THE PATH
## ON THE RIGHT HAND SIDE OF THE COLLECTION OF
## LAWSON CYPRESS

Near the path is the unmistakeable sharply tapering
trunk of a Redwood - not one of the North American
ones but the Chinese Dawn Redwood. Near the top of
this group of trees a Leyland Cypress reminds us just
how large this very popular tree can grow and this one
is still gaining height.

At the next cul-de-sac the Giant Sequoia that appeared
in front of the B.A.T. building when viewed from
Firgrove can be seen taking up most of the front garden
of No.38. When planted, it was some 170 yards west of
Goldsworth House, the headquarters of Mr.Slocock's
Goldsworth Nursery. The historic house with much
character was retained as a prestigous office by New
Ideal Homes until almost the last phase of their
building works on Goldsworth Park. It was then pulled
down ignominiously to make way for Badgers Close.

The Giant Sequoia is known in Britain as the Wellingtonia.
This derives from the first description of the tree
in the Gardeners Chronicle of December 1853 wherein
John Lindley named it Wellingtonia gigantea in honour
of the Duke of Wellington who had died the year before.
Enraged Americans countered with Taxodium
Washingtonianum and Washingtonia californica. They
pointed out that their George Washington at least liked
trees which our Duke of Wellington reputedly did not.

The name Wellingtonia was retained in Britain at, it is
said, the insistance of Queen Victoria who wanted our
national hero to be so honoured. The botanical name
was settled eventually in 1938 as Sequoiadendron
giganteum.

In terms of weight of timber this is the largest **plant**
on Earth (the Coast Redwood is taller and the Baob has
a greater girth). This particular specimen was planted
about 1880 and is now 19.5m high; its full-grown
American counterparts are four times higher with a
main stem of the same diameter as the whole spread of
this tree. (see also p.21)

RETURN FROM THE CUL-DE-SAC PART OF INGLEWOOD
AND CROSS THE ROAD BY ALLOWAY CLOSE

On the way admire another reminder of the former nursery - the fine Beech hedge (right of the photograph below) and the line of Lawson Cypress behind the garages of Milcombe Close. Several of the many Lawson Cypress cultivars are of local origin, such as 'Erecta' which was raised in Knaphill in 1855 and 'Green Spire' which was raised by Jackmans before 1947.

On the other side of Milcombe Close, outside No.5 is the blue spire of a Smooth Arizona Cypress, Cupressus glabra, introduced from Central Arizona in 1907. It is valuable for being able to withstand drought. It can also be clipped into hedges but looks more striking as seen here, as a free-standing specimen tree. This particular one is not the largest in Britain but, nevertheless, has a significant girth of 5'8" (I.73m).

CONTINUE AHEAD TOWARDS STAINTON WALK

On the right is the Cedar noted from Firgrove. At first sight the level branching might encourage you to think it is a Cedar of Lebanon but the drooping tips reveal it is a Deodar. On the left, a large Corsican Pine makes an outstanding landmark and more carefully selected species need planting in the right places to perpetuate the landscape value of pines

In Colyton Close, outside Nos.9 and 11, is a Vine-leaf
Maple, Acer cissifolium, from Japan. It can be readily
identified by its wire-thin stalks to its three leaflets.
It is one of the more unusual of the 130 species and
numerous cultivars of Maple.

## TURN RIGHT AND CROSS WINNINGTON WAY

On the right hand side, at the bottom of the garden
between the 2nd and 3rd house is a more interesting
pine. The species can be grouped according to the
number of needles with a common base. The native
Scots Pine has its needles in pairs. This pine has
them in fives and is most likely a Bhutan Pine.

Above - the Blue Atlas Cedar, planted in the late 1970s
near the junction with St Johns Road. Beyond can be
seen a sample of many areas of the Park that is being
planted up with trees and shrubs for the future. In
both public spaces and private gardens the great range
of colour and form provided by conifers is being fully
explored. Some will need thinning out in the future.

## TURN LEFT, CROSS ST JOHNS ROAD AND TURN RIGHT
## INTO JANNOWAY HILL ROAD

Walk up this unmade road taking the right fork at a
large Holly tree. After the housing estate this walk
through the woods makes a pleasant change and also
introduces another species – the Sweet Chestnut, that
makes up much of the wood. It does well on sandy
soils and provides valuable timber. It also makes
a fine specimen tree but is rarely planted as such.
Another important timber tree is the Douglas Fir,
at the top on the left, with its pendulous branches
enhanced with a strong hint of silver. Next to it
is a huge Red Oak.

## TURN RIGHT AND CONTINUE ALONG FIRBANK LANE

On the left, screening the railway line, is a dense
undisturbed woodland of Oak, Sweet Chestnut and
Scots Pine. This is not only a valuable wildlife
habitat but a linear green corridor that enriches
this area.

## TURN RIGHT AT ST JOHNS HILL ROAD
## AND RIGHT AGAIN INTO HOLLY CLOSE

The close is named after the evergreen Holly Oak at the
end of the road. There are some 300 species of evergreen oak but this one is a hybrid, between the Cork
and Turkey Oaks. It is known as the Lucombe Oak, Quercus
x hispanica 'Lucombeana', having originated in Lucombe's
nursery at Exeter between 1763 and 1830. It is of
value as a screening tree, not only because it can reach
a great size but because it will retain its leaves long
after other deciduous trees have lost theirs, unless
the weather is severe.

Returning to the entrance of the close, look back to
enjoy the Blue Atlas Cedar, Swamp Cypress and Weeping
Beech on the far side of the road which all help to
make up Woking's rich tree heritage.

## ST JOHNS HILL ROAD

Opposite 'Barricane' is an impressive columnar tree
with upward sweeping branches, in the grounds of
'Deerside'. This is the Incense Cedar noted from
Inglewood, taking its name from the scent of its

crushed leaves. It is not a true Cedar though, but was given that name by American colonists to make its timber more marketable. It is native of Oregon and California and was introduced to Britain in 1853. Its scented wood can be worked smoothly so it is the wood favoured for making pencils.

Firgrove probably got its name from the line of five Coast Redwoods from here to The Mount. Seedling Coast Redwoods and a Grand Fir have been planted on the right hand verge to perpetuate this association.

Between the 4th and 5th Coast Redwood has been squeezed the main access to The Mount, past a Deodar Cedar and a pollarded Wellingtonia. Both of these are now suffering from the lowering of the water table. The Wellingtonia is very unusual because, although the Coast Redwood will regenerate from a stump, the Wellingtonia rarely does, yet this has six main stems. It was featured strongly when photographs were taken for architectural awards when development here was nearing completion.

On the other side of St.Johns Hill Road is a bungalow called 'Cedar Ridge' and directly behind the apex of the garage can be glimpsed another of Jackman's mature Tulip Trees. Further down, on the boundary of St Johns Hill House, towering above everything else, is the finest Giant Sequoia in the district. It can be seen well from Winston Churchill School and from the roundabout at the bottom of Amstel Way.

Lastly, as the description ends at Woodend Close, note the fine young Douglas Fir reaching for the sky outside 'Merton'. It is now old enough to be bearing its very distinctive cones with their three-pronged bracts projecting like tongues. This tree will soon be playing an important part in maintaining the character of St Johns as all living things have a finite life and we should be taking every opportunity to plant similar forest species, rather than for ever opting for small ornamentals. What will St Johns look like in a hundred years if we do not?

CONTINUE AHEAD TO RETURN TO THE STARTING POINT

# HORSELL

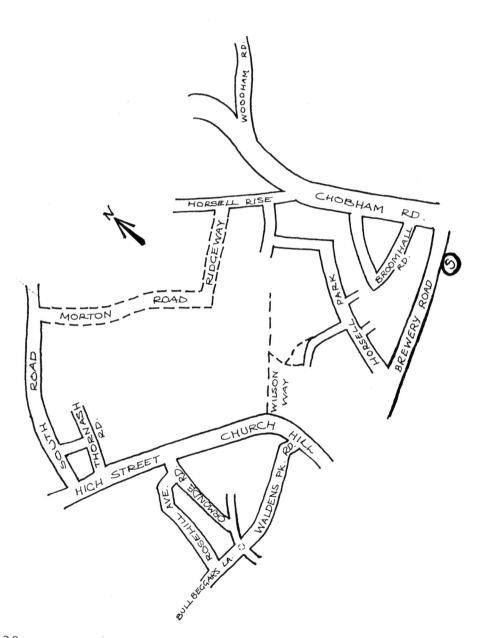

RAMBLE AREA 3

HORSELL

STARTING AT BREWERY ROAD CAR PARK - Look across
the car park to its boundary with Kingswood Court and
you'll see a line of four trees.  They are all oaks, of
two different species, out of some 500 that are to be
found in the Northern Hemisphere.  Only two of them
are native to Britain - the English Oak which has leaves
with hardly any stalk but long stalks for its acorns and
the Sessile Oak which has stalks for its leaves but not
for its acorns.  One of the four trees here is an English
Oak, which is to be expected in this area; the Sessile
Oak is uncommon in S.E.England.

The other three oaks are all Turkey Oaks and easily
distinguished because they have jagged leaves instead
of roundly lobed ones. Also, the acorn cups are not
bald like English and Sessile Oaks but have a covering
of little growths to make them 'mossy'.  The Turkey Oak
was introduced from Turkey by the Exeter nurseryman,
J.Lucombe, in 1735.  It is now found frequently as a
wild tree in the Surrey countryside.

Where Turkey and English Oaks grow together Knopper Galls
can be found.  These are acorns that have hosted the
grub of a gall wasp and in so doing have developed out
of shape with spikey distortions. They will never grow
into oak trees. Both species are needed because the gall
wasp transfers from one to the other during its life
cycle.  The eggs are laid in the catkins of the Turkey
Oak and wasps from these lay eggs in the acorns of the
English Oak and these in due course return to the Turkey
Oaks.

The line of trees along the Brewery Road frontage of the
car park are Small-leaved Limes.  This is a native tree
that once, say back in Saxon times, was the dominant
tree in many of the woodlands.  Since then it has
declined into a scarcity in the wild. As an ornamental,
however, it is regularly planted.  It has the advantage
over the Common Lime in that its smaller heart-shaped
leaves do not attract the aphids that drip 'honey dew'.

## LOOK FOR THE BLOCK OF FLATS BESIDE TREES OPPOSITE THE CAR PARK. TAKE THE PATH BESIDE THE FLATS THROUGH THE TREES.

You will pass two Sweet Chestnut trees. It is thought that this tree was originally introduced by the Romans, who enjoyed its chestnuts. Since then it has been an important timber tree and one of Surrey's important trees for coppicing. The coppice stools produced valuable crops of small round wood with many uses, including the pales for 'chestnut fencing'.

Next on the right an English and Holly Oak grow side by side. The Holly or Holm Oak comes from the Mediterranean and holds its leaves throughout the winter. In early summer it is covered with yellow catkins, followed by the new silvery green leaves.

The woodland on the left is mainly Oak and in the spring the margin is a carpet of bluebells – a sure sign that the wood is of great age. At the top of the rise, where the footpath crosses, a Wellingtonia can be seen above the flats of Graylands on the right.

## CROSS THE ROAD INTO THE FOOTPATH OPPOSITE

This path follows an ancient boundary, indicated by the stools of hazel on the right (photo below). Their great girth indicates considerable age and this together with the remnant of Oakwood under which they were normally coppiced all indicate an old tradition of woodsmanship in this district of Woking.

On the inside of the bend is a line of Monterey Cypress, Cupressus macrocarpa. The macrocarpa part of its name means it has large fruits and if you look up you will see the bunches of spherical cones, larger than those on the other Cupressus species along these rambles. The Monterey part of its name comes from Monterey in California near which, on a peninsular now called Cypress Point, this tree found a refuge from the Ice Age glaciers. There it survived as small trees, tolerant of the salt-laden winds, but when the ice retreated it was unable to spread northwards again, being stranded on its peninsular. Away from these conditions it is able to grow naturally tall, as it does in this country and is a parent of the popular and tall Leyland Cypress.

Although some distance away, it is worth looking across to St.Andrew's Prep. School which has a worthy tree collection in its grounds. Two in particular are noteworthy. One is the maginificent example of a Cedar of Lebanon with its spreading branches, which was first introduced into this country about 1640. Most of those early introductions perished in the winter of 1740 which was so severe that Frost Fairs were held on the frozen River Thames. The other tree to note is the Tulip Tree to the left and which is probably the largest in the district. This is an introduction from the United States where it is grown commercially for its timber, known as 'whitewood'.

## CONTINUE TO THE END OF THE FOOTPATH

At the end are three large trunks of Black Poplar which is an European species. It will hybridise with American species and in that country they are called Cottonwoods after the heavy coating of white cottony down surrounding the seeds to aid wind dispersal.

## LEFT ALONG WILSON WAY

On the left an avenue of Norway Maples contrasts with Purple Plum while along the boundary of the churchyard a series of Cherries provide an outstanding but brief display of white and pink blossom in the spring.

The trees in this area suffered badly in the storm of January 1990 but fortunately one of the mature Corsican Pines survived. It's the one at the end of the road, outside the school where it makes such a feature but where it also makes the buildings look smaller, helping to keep a village character in Horsell. Sadly it is taken too much for granted - its future replacement should be growing now. This feature is too good to lose.(below)

## ENTER THE CHURCHYARD THROUGH THE IRON GATE

The huge tree with four large trunks is a Beech. Further to the left is a variegated white-leaved Highclere Holly which takes its name from Highclere Castle, Berkshire, where this hybrid was first raised. To the right is a Strawberry Tree, Arbutus unedo. Its fruits do indeed look like strawberries but they are not exactly tasty. Unedo is derived from 'unus' - one, and 'edo' - to eat. You only eat one! It is always a small tree and keeps its bark pale in colour by peeling. In spring the dark pink shoots bear white flowers like those of the lily-of-the-valley.

## RETURN TO, AND CONTINUE ALONG, WILSON WAY

## TURN LEFT INTO CHURCH HILL

Just as the churchyard already visited is rich with a variety of trees and glorious for a brief spell in the spring when the Cherry trees are in blossom, so round here in front of the church the setting is rewarding. Spring blossom is provided again but this time by the Snowy Mespil (Amelanchier) which is grown in many of the gardens and provides colour again in the autumn when the foliage turns a brilliant red.

The trees around the church itself make a prominent feature, not only along the approach roads, but visible from the centre of Woking aswell. Bright green leaves of Robinia contrast with the dark Corsican Pines and Holly Oaks enlivened by the yellow fastigiate Irish Yews by the lychgate. Crowning all is the massive Blue Atlas Cedar next to the church tower, which although damaged, has survived the great storms. (Illustrated below and as the frontispiece.)

## GO DOWN CHURCH HILL AND TURN RIGHT INTO WALDENS PARK ROAD

On the right is a thick mixed hedge, composed mostly of Holly, Elm and Yew, making an important landscape feature. Then, on the bend, there are two Copper Beeches. These are followed by an avenue of London Planes which do so well in street conditions. Planes can become massive trees but still serve well in such suburban streets as this because they respond well to pollarding, giving all the benefits of height without the disadvantages of low spreading boughs. That has been done here and also to the Ash-leaved Maple outside No.9. However, the cuts can become infected and then rot sets in. Indeed a cavity has developed in the Plane outside No.6. which is now sporting an Oak sapling. Presumably a squirrel or jay dropped an acorn down into the cavity. (Illustrated opposite)

## CROSS THE ROUNDABOUT INTO BULLBEGGARS LANE TURN RIGHT INTO ROSEHILL AVENUE

Starting on the corner of Bullbeggars Lane there is a Hornbeam - horn meaning hard (timber used for the cogs in windmills and now for butchers' blocks) and beam from an old word for timber trees.

Outside No.12. is the unmistakeable yellow leaved Robinia pseudoacacia 'Frisia', introduced to trade about 1950 and already extremely popular. This tree only turns green in very hot summers.

At the bend by No.44 are two more evergreen Oaks. The one with the smoother bark, almost black, is another Holm or Holly Oak of which there are quite a number in and around Woking. The other, with the very craggy bark is much rarer. It is a Cork Oak, Quercus suber. This is the Oak that in Spain and Portugal has its bark stripped off to provide cork. This leaves the trunks dark red but the inner layers and cambium is left unharmed so that it regrows and can be cut again. It is remarkable that this tree with a range that spreads into North Africa can adapt so well to a pavement in Horsell.

In fact it is hardy right to the north of Scotland. Where the Woking tree becomes so special is in the way it has indeed grown up into a tree whereas so often in Britain it tends to flop its lower branches down onto the ground and become a dull mound. To see good upright specimens one would expect to go to Cornwall.

Above – the Holly Oak or Holm Oak behind the Cork Oak, making a strong feature on the bend in Rosehill Avenue. The Cork Oak is seen sprouting well after surgery.

Below – a closer view of the beautifully figured and sculptured bark of the Cork Oak that provides the familiar cork in everyday use.

## TURN LEFT INTO THE HIGH STREET

Outside the shop on the left contrast the large foliage of the Copper Beech with the smaller foliage of the Purple Plum, that forms an avenue along much of the High Street. They give a welcome but brief display of white blossom in spring; sadly, some were lost during the great storms of January 1990.

Over on the right, Horsell Way displays some of the wide range of Norway Maples, from yellow to deep copper.

## TURN RIGHT INTO THORNASH ROAD AND THEN TURN LEFT INTO THORNASH WAY

In complete contrast to the 'red' foliage just noted, there is now an avenue of Whitebeams which have almost silver leaves when the buds first break and which are pale underneath for the rest of the season. This is one of our few native trees of the chalk downlands of southern England and belongs to the same genus, Sorbus, as the Rowan or Mountain Ash. The genus contains over 80 species, numerous hybrids and cultivars, some of which were bred in Surrey. As street trees the County's collection has been highlighted by the Forestry Commission as being of national importance; we have a duty to safeguard it.

As small trees of ornamental value they are popular for planting in new development areas but it is important to keep a balance and vary the scale. Here, it is good to see how large trees, such as the plane and the two limes, have been accommodated into the gardens of the flats at the junction with South Road.

## TURN RIGHT INTO SOUTH ROAD

Along on the right hand side are four River Birches, Betula nigra. The nigra part comes from the very dark bark which makes them unusual among birches. There is a Silver Birch growing in the line which gives a useful opportunity for comparing the two. The River Birch comes from the Eastern United States and is not at all common in this country and as a street tree like this, is very rare. (Photograph next page)

47

Above - the rare River Birch. These particular ones
are, unfortunately, infected with fungi which fruit
rather too bountifully around the bases in the
autumn. The branches are dying back and many have
been removed but even so, the days of these trees are
numbered. As they are believed to have been planted
by one of the local nurserymen they are an important
part of Woking's tree heritage and it would be good if
new ones could be planted on a site free of the fungus.

On the left is the edge of Horsell Common - an area of
Special Scientific Interest. All the remaining areas
of heathland in S.E.England are under threat from the
regeneration of birch, pine and then oak and so this is
a site where it is important to restrict tree growth.
These types of heathland habitat are only found along
the Atlantic fringe of N.W.Europe, from Sweden down to
Portugal so they are of world importance. This has only
been realised fully in recent years and efforts are now
being made to save such habitats and here at Horsell
such measures are especially important if we are to
keep its very rare species. The heathlands of each
country vary slightly and so there is nowhere else in
the world that is EXACTLY like these English heaths.

## TURN RIGHT INTO MORTON ROAD

On the school boundary is a line of Norway Maples - a typical example of unimaginative planting, although in the centre of the school frontage is a purple strain raised locally and known as 'Goldsworth Purple'. It's yet another reminder of the world-wide importance of the part played by local nurseries in establishing new trees and shrubs.

At the end of the Maple line English Elms are shooting rapidly to re-establish themselves. Enjoy them before another outbreak of Dutch Elm Disease takes its toll and there will almost certainly be another outbreak; it has been happening since the Middle Ages at least. At the first access there are four Ash trees and two contrasting Willows.

There are some 300 species of Willows and numerous hybrids, making them a difficult group to sort out. These two are more distinctive than many. The one with bright green glossy leaves is the Crack Willow and the one with smaller blue-grey leaves is the White Willow.

Lyndhurst Close on the left reminds us of the Lime or Linden Trees that have given their names to towns like Lyndhurst, Lindfield and Lindford. There are two native Limes in Britain, the Broad-leaved and the Small-leaved but the size of leaf is not very helpful; better to remember that the Broad-leaved has hairy leaves and the Small-leaved has heart-shaped leaves. There is a third Lime, the Common Lime, which is a hybrid between the other two and can usually be distinguished by extensive sprouting at the base of the trunk. For confirmation, the leaves are not hairy and are usually shiny with honeydew from aphids. They often get little bright red growths on them which are nail galls.

Lime trees are called Basswoods in America - the bass coming from the fibrous inner bark, used for tying garden plants. Russian peasants made shoes from it and the Vikings made ropes from it for their ship rigging.

On the corner of Lyndhurst Close a semi-mature Norway
Spruce shows the dramatic effect of Spruce Aphids
which attacked in 1988-89. Numbers had been able to
build up due to several mild winters so that this was
the worst year on record. The aphid attacks the older
needles causing them to fall and leave the inside of
the tree quite bare. New growth at the tips will help
to shield this for although such an attack will not
kill the tree it will slow growth considerably.

An unusual sight is the line of Deodar Cedars that mark
the boundary of 'Pine Trees' on the left. They have all
been pollarded. Opposite, by 'Deepdale' are two Small-
Leaved Limes with their small heart-shaped leaves. Then
outside 'Lyndhurst Lodge' (lime again!) on the left, are
five Nootka Cypress, Chamaecyparis nootkatensis 'Pendula'.
They get their unusual name from being discovered at
Nootka on Vancouver Island in 1888. Their importance lies
in them being one of the parents of the famous Leyland
Cypress.

## FOLLOW THE ROAD LEFT INTO THE RIDGEWAY
## TURN LEFT INTO RIDGEWAY GARDENS

By 'Little Wissett' the golden foliage of Robinia
pseudoacacia 'Frisia' looks well against the blue
foliage of the six Blue Atlas Cedars. Both the blue
and the green forms of the latter are native to the
Atlas Mountains of North Africa. From Central Arizona
come the two conifers set neatly on either side of
the driveway to No.11. They are Cupressus glabra, the
Arizona Cypress, with upright blue-grey foliage,
smelling of grapefruit when crushed.

On the right, near the bottom of the hill, the garden
of 'Hillrise' has an Old World collection of trees
including the Walnut, Juglans regia, introduced from
S.E.Europe by the Romans who named it Juglans which
comes from Jovis glans - the nuts of Jovis or Jupiter.
The Saxons called it Walnut from their Old English
wealh knutu meaning foreign nut. From nearer home
comes the Strawberry Tree from the counties of Kerry ·
and Cork in Ireland while the nearby Weeping Cherry
comes all the way from the Far East - China and Japan.

## RETURN TO THE RIDGEWAY AND TURN LEFT

Outside 'Music Water' is a young Douglas Fir, with short, soft, dense needles. Its botanical name is Pseudotsuga menziesii which commemorates Archibald Menzies who first 'discovered' the tree on Captain Vancouver's expedition in 1792. Its English name commemorates David Douglas, an intrepid Scot from Old Scone, Perthshire, who was the first to send seeds to Britain.

By the road hump, 'Little Upton' has a young Dawn Redwood, the 'living fossil' tree noted outside Woking Park in the first ramble. It is a deciduous conifer, discovered in China in 1941 and introduced to Britain in 1948. It makes a shapely, conic tree with attractive yellow-green foliage that turns a good autumn colour.

A fine example of an evergreen conifer is the huge three-stemmed Lawson Cypress outside 'Manor Croft'. This was introduced from the USA by Lawson's Nursery in 1894. People often forget how valuable is the dense growth of such conifers for providing our little garden birds with shelter; without it the smaller species succumb to the cold and wet of an English winter.

By the next road hump Common Walnuts are progressing well into making a feature in the road. It is always good to see young trees coming on, dispelling the myth that they grow slowly. That is only true when they are under stress, as for example, when large stock is moved with too little root or when the site has been prepared inadequately.

## TURN RIGHT INTO HORSELL RISE

Along at Church Road on the right admire the open-grown native Scots Pine with its orange-coloured bark, making a good feature tree. Its natural habit of losing its lower branches enables many plants to be grown in the garden area below it. Where there is enough space this is a tree that can add much character to an area.

Also in this garden of 'West Herne' are two Incense Cedars, Calocedrus decurrens, originating from Oregon and California. There, in the wild, it has a sparse spreading habit but in Britain it is very different. As you can see, it makes a narrow columnar crown with a rounded top and has its small branches sweeping up rather than spreading out.

At 'Derryneen', on the right an unusual Weeping Blue Atlas Cedar. It was some 2m high in 1989 but should grow rapidly. In contrast, near the bottom of the hill, a huge Red Oak has spread its branches almost to the centre of the road. It gets its name from the way its leaves turn a brilliant red in autumn, in its native America, but here the colour is considerably more variable. Various American Oaks are called Red Oaks. This one is Quercus rubra, but to see an avenue of mixed Red Oaks try the one that leads to the totem pole in Windsor Great Park.

## TURN RIGHT INTO CHOBHAM ROAD

The conifers outside of 'Laleham Court' are mostly the Lawson Cypress but there are also two Western Red Cedars, Thuja plicata. They are readily distinguished by their cones: the Lawson Cypress has little pea-like cones whereas the Western Red Cedars are ovoid and stand about one centimeter high. The latter is not a true Cedar; if it was it would be in the genus Cedrus and not Thuja, but it got the name as a ploy to help market its timber when it was discovered in America around the time of the Gold Rush. It has superb timber for long straight needs, such as ladder poles, rugby posts and even the totem pole in Windsor Great Park. Its specific name of plicata refers to its plaited scale-like leaves but you have to look carefully or else use a lens in order to see them.

## TURN RIGHT INTO THURLTON COURT

A short detour here will reveal an oddity (on the left), the Corkscrew Willow, Salix matsudana 'Tortuosa'. This is a strange variant of the Peking Willow which has its branches 'tortured' into contorted shapes which show up most interestingly when bare of leaves in the winter. Several trees have this distorted habit, which gardeners seem to love or hate, including the Common Hazel.

## RETURN TO CHOBHAM ROAD AND TURN RIGHT

Just past Broomhall Road, 'Bradstock' has one of the most unusual trees on earth - the Maidenhair Tree, Ginko biloba, with its two lobed leaves. Ginkos were the dominant form of tree some 200 million years ago and have not evolved into either broadleaf or conifer. It was found by Europeans in Japan but is native only of China. It makes a slender tree, often like this one in having a bifurcated trunk at about 4m from the ground. In autumn the leaves turn a bright yellow before falling.

## TURN RIGHT INTO BREWERY ROAD TO RETURN TO THE STARTING POINT

# MAYBURY

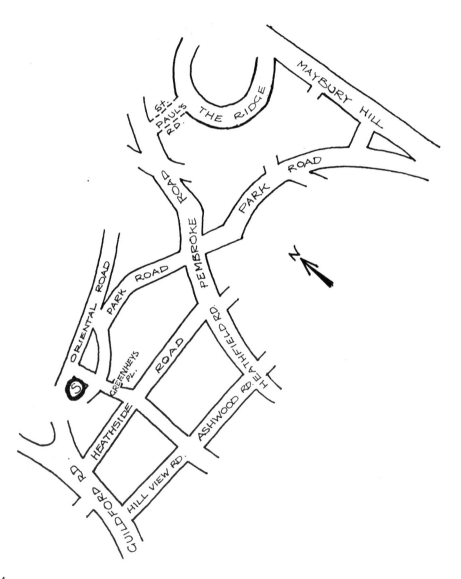

RAMBLE AREA 4

HEATHSIDE AND MAYBURY

STARTING AT THE HEATHSIDE CRESCENT CAR PARK

The car park is a building of which the Borough Council
can be duly proud. The local Oriental connections are
reflected in its sweeping arches and tile-hung facades,
all making a welcome change from the boring concrete
norm for such buildings. It also provides an ideal
vantage point from which to look out over the district
to appreciate the value of the tree cover.

The building is aligned east-west so it is easy to
give directions. To help get a sense of place, the
radio mast visible from the NW tower is 8 miles away
at Camberley while the range of hills visible from
the SE tower is the Hog's Back.

Closer at hand, the SW tower enables us to look down
onto one of the problem sites for trees in the town
centre. You can look down onto the former Boys'
Grammar School, now converted into Magistrates Courts
and if you know Woking you will remember that the
site was shielded by trees. Whether the Borough
Council would have liked to retain these or not, they
had to be removed at the insistence of the Home Office
we were told. Ironically a Robinia has now been
left to germinate and grow on the other side of the
fence, in Calluna Court. Notice also, a huge tree
in the garden of St.Andrew's Church – a Liquidamber,
which turns a brilliant gold and then red before it
loses its leaves.

LEAVE FROM THE S.E.TOWER, CROSS WHITE ROSE
LANE INTO GREENHEYS PLACE

The holly hedge is the thing to note here. When the
houses were built in the 1960s it was claimed that
this length of hedge was all that remained marking
the boundary of land once owned by wealthy solicitor,
Mr.Rastrict, who held extensive land on this south
side.

It is part of Woking's folklore that it was his refusal to sell land that prevented the development of the town on this south side of the railway. That story does not stand close scrutiny but Rastrict was important in creating the character of this district.

His residence, Woking Lodge, was surrounded by either a high wall or a hedge. This is claimed to be part of that hedge and part of the wall still runs beside the footpath from the station to the Oriental Road car park. Set into this wall is a plaque on which his name is spelt backwards.

In the grass verge behind the hedge are several Swedish Whitebeams, leaning at all angles. This is all too common, particularly with Sorbus. Large nursery stock is planted with a dense heavy crown and all too little root to support it. The botanic name. Sorbus intermedia refers to the lobed leaf that is inter-mediate between the entire leaf of the Whitebeam and the compound leaf of the Rowan.

At the end of the path an English Oak shows how a large branch should be removed, such that a collar is left on the trunk. This collar can then generate a healing process that can be seen taking place. If the cut is made too close to the trunk this process does not occur, leaving the wound unable to heal and open to decay. No surgeon should make a flush cut.

## TURN RIGHT INTO HEATHSIDE ROAD

Along the boundary of the church is a line of Yew trees which have long been associated with churches. Pre-Christian peoples made gifts of evergreen boughs at their mid-winter festival; Druids placed evergreen branches about their homes to offer winter harbour to the tree spirits.

The notion that Yews were grown in churchyards to yield material for medieval archers is not true. English bowmen used material from Spain, Italy and Portugal where the warmer climate produced timber with a harder texture and a finer grain. When these countries placed an embargo on its export Lombard

Bankers were compelled by the Government to deliver a
certain quantity of foreign Yew staves with every cask
of Greek or Italian wine admitted to the London Custom
House. Great amounts were needed. For example, in 1356
Edward III instructed sheriffs to supply 240,000 'good'
arrows for one of his campaigns.

Look down the driveway of the Vicarage for a different
view of the Liquidamber and note the Corsican Pines
beyond, that give a good setting to the decked car park.
Several were lost during construction and more again in
the January 1990 gales, but by request a few more
seedlings have been planted. Continuing development
along this road is eroding gradually the tree screen,
although it is good to see that when Crest built
Hawksmoore Place in 1989 they made a token planting
of one Corsican Pine. The whole area abounds with
Robinia, which is successfully seeding to regenerate
in several communal corners. What will happen to the
other mature trees along here - Douglas Fir, Deodar
Cedar, Western Red Cedar, Monterey Pine, Incense Cedar,
etc. - during the next phase of development?

## TURN LEFT INTO GUILDFORD ROAD

In the centre of the road one has to admire the
tenacity of the London Plane to survive in such
conditions. Sadly the Plane and the Beech tree
at Phillips Quadrant are losing their fight for life.
Here, some fine examples of Red Oaks at their peak
and so it is time to plant for their eventual
replacement. At Hill View Road look towards the
Cotterage Hotel to admire the effect created by the
tall forest trees - Holly, Douglas Fir and Monterey
Cypress - an effect that should be borne in mind when
new planting is being proposed. The current fashion
for planting smaller ornamental trees such as Prunus
and Malus will never soften and screen such views to
the same extent, if at all.

## TURN LEFT INTO HILL VIEW ROAD

In places such as Fairview Avenue some of the original
Larch, Oak, Red Oak and Horse Chestnut remain. These
trees are more in scale with the large surrounding

flats. At Park Drive, two large Cedars survive from the original Victorian gardens. At the bottom of the hill by the access to the garages, a group of pines shows what an important part such trees can play. Similarly, the corner at White Rose Lane is dominated by two fine Corsican Pines.

On the far side of the road another Liquidamber and next to it is a Judas Tree. Ancient legend says that Judas Escariot hanged himself from a branch of this tree after betraying Christ. This beautiful, bushy tree certainly grows in Israel, aswell as many other Mediterranean lands. At Easter time it bears a wealth of purple blossoms in clusters which are unusual for springing not just from the twigs but out of the branches and even the trunk. The petals were used formerly to sweeten salads when sugar was rare. The leaves are also attractive being kidney-shaped and bluish green.

In Woking we are indeed fortunate to be able to grow trees from every continent of the world. From Australia comes the bluish green tree across the road, which is a Eucalyptus, a Cider Gum, that makes whole forests in Australia. In their early years they hold all records for fast growth and even in Woking's climate can increase by some 2m a year. This is partly because they do not stop growing in the winter but simply pause when it is very cold. Only in the very severest of winters are they killed. These are the world's tallest broadleaved trees and in Britain their height has now reached over 30m. They are adapted to grow in dry conditions; each leaf has a waxy coat to reduce water loss and inside are the famous aromatic oils, distilled for perfumes and cough cures.

Towering over the rear of the houses in Pembroke Gardens are examples of another tree with interesting height records. These are Monterey Cypresses which only grow to small trees in their native Monterey district of California. Planted elsewhere they grow up to statures like these. They are more often seen at the south coast because they are very resistant to salt scorching, unlike to many other trees.

On the left, outside 'Fairbanks', a huge Copper Beech partners a less familiar tree on the other side of the driveway. This is a Black Mulberry; its name referring to the colour of its fruits which look like raspberries. This is not a native tree but has been cultivated for so long that the date of its introduction is unknown. They grow rapidly in Southern England but not usually to a height above 6m. Due to their naturally gnarled trunks they often give a false impression of great age.

Mulberry trees are the famed food of silkworms and James I organised the mass growing of the trees to support a native silk industry (locally, at Weybridge) but for various reasons it did not succeed. This was partly due to the planting of Black Mulberries when the silk worms prefer the White Mulberry.

Black Mulberries in cultivation are usually female as they can ripen edible berries without males. The seeds, however, are infertile, so the tree has to be propagated by cuttings, called truncheons, which are taken in winter a metre long and a thumb thick. These are set halfway into the ground.

A few yards further, on the same side of the road, is a huge Pin Oak - one of the four species of Red Oak from North America that are likely to be met with. This one has more deeply lobed leaves than the Red Oak proper, already noted on the rambles, but not so deeply lobed as the Scarlet Oak. All have a rather smooth bark with clear trunks. Opposite, for contrasting foliage, there is a Copper Norway Maple, a Sweet Chestnut and a Common Walnut.

## TURN RIGHT INTO PARK ROAD

Outside No.42 there's the golden foliage of a Sawara Cypress with the challenging botanic name: Chamaecyparis pisifera 'Filifera Aurea'. The pisifera part means pea bearing which refers to the cones which are like small wrinkled peas. Filifera refers to the wire-like shoots of the foliage.

On the opposite side of the road, between Nos.44 & 46, there is a Tree of Heaven, Ailanthus altissima, from Northern China. Its name is a poetic translation of Tree of the Skies,(altissima means very tall). Its compound leaves can be nearly a metre long, with 20 pairs of leaflets which have 1-3 teeth at their base - a unique feature. In autumn the leaflets fall first to be followed by their stems later.

In June and July these trees carry large panicles of greenish white flowers but each tree is either wholly male or wholly female. In September the female trees have bright orange-red seeds hanging in clusters of golden keys high above the green foliage. These do not make a nuisance of themselves as they are rarely viable in Britain although it is in Southern Europe and the Eastern United States where it is becoming naturalised. It also spreads vigorously by strong suckers from the roots.

It is a most attractive tree with its smooth dark grey bark with grey veining. This together with its bold leaves of almost sub-tropical appearance make the tree worthy of being more widely planted.

**TURN LEFT INTO SYLVAN CLOSE, KEEP STRAIGHT ON THROUGH THE NARROW FOOTPATH AND TURN LEFT AT MAYBURY HILL**

On the left, in the front garden of 'Conifers' are three Scots Pines with their distinctive orange bark. As its name implies, this is a native but its range extends down to Spain and right out to Eastern Siberia. Contrast these with the dark trunks of the Corsican Pines in the grounds of St.Columba's House on the opposite side of the road.

**AT THE TOP OF THE HILL TURN LEFT INTO THE RIDGE**

More Robinia are germinating along the left of this hilltop route. On the outside of the bend in the road is 'Maybury Knowle' where for some years lived George Bernard Shaw - enjoying the view but not walks in the woods!

## TURN LEFT INTO UNMADE ST PAULS ROAD
## AT THE BOTTOM TURN LEFT INTO PEMBROKE ROAD

Almost opposite, in the fork between this road and
Onslow Crescent is a house named after its Chile Pine.
This is the alternative name for the Monkey Puzzle
Tree which got its odd name from a remark made by a
visitor to the Pencarrow Gardens in Cornwall, who
said it would puzzle a monkey if it tried to climb
one, hence its earlier name of Monkey Puzzler.

Sweeping up from the flat roof, the boughs here make an
especially effective feature, especially in winter when
the foil of the deciduous trees is absent.

It was first discovered by the Spaniards who had
settled in Chile in 1780. While visiting Valpariso
in 1795, Archibald Menzies, the ship's surgeon and
botanist, was intrigued by the nuts served as a
desert at a banquet being given by the Governor.
He pocketed a few seeds, germinated them on board
ship and presented the small trees to Joseph Banks
of Kew when the ship returned. Later, William Lobb
collected a large consignment of seed for Veitch's
Nursery at Exeter in 1844.

Its botanic name is Araucaria araucana after the
Araucaria Indians who found many uses for this tree.
They ground the nuts for flour or roasted them like
chestnuts and used the resin as a plaster and in
medicines. The timber is a useful softwood with a
cream coloured softwood zone with tiny knots in it.
In South America it is used extensively for building,
fencing and packaging. The timber of a related tree,
Araucaria brasiliana, is exported regularly to
Europe and North America as Parana Pine.

Male and female flowers appear on separate trees; this
one is a male. Look for the flowers in May. They are
yellowish cylindrical cones. Female flowers will
expand into small green 'pineapples' which take two
years to mature. They then turn brown and break up to
release a large brown seed from behind each scale.

**CONTINUE ALONG PEMBROKE ROAD AND TURN RIGHT
INTO PARK ROAD**

Pass the huge Sweet Chestnut on the left and continue
a little further to take a short detour into Downside
Orchard. Outside the Mount Green Housing Association
is the needle-like Juniper'Skyrocket', while at the
end of the road it is good to see that the Larch,
Douglas Fir and Holly Oak have been carefully kept.

Returning to Park Road admire a Coast Redwood outside
No.30. This Californian tree is claimed to be the
tallest tree in the world, obtaining heights over 112m.

In this rich treescape there is a curiosum; the lamp
post at the junction of Coley Avenue. It is one of
Woking's originals, being first run on gas until the
creation of the Urban District Council in 1895. They
promptly converted them to electricity, being one of
the first Councils to have electric lighting. When
they wanted to extend the system in 1905 they were
not satisfied with the performance of the electricity
company and had them converted back to gas; ironically
they used second-hand parts from Battersea Council
who were converting their lighting to electricity.

Above - the historic lamp from the days when this whole
district was new development, with large gardens along
curving streets. Today that housing is shielded by the
collection of mature forest trees throughout the area.
In addition, the gardens have filled out with an even
greater range of trees and shrubs, making the entire
district a rewarding place to explore. Will Goldsworth
Park look like this in a hundred years time ?

## AT THE END OF PARK ROAD TURN LEFT INTO HEATHSIDE CRESCENT

Passing under a spreading Red Oak on the left, we
are brought back to the car park from where the
ramble commenced. This walk is particularly worthwhile in the spring because of all the beautiful
Magnolia blossoms in the gardens.

# EXPLORING FURTHER AROUND SURREY

**N.W.SURREY - 10 TOWN AND COUNTRY RAMBLES**
Includes Chobham and Cobham and the areas around Staines, Chertsey and Weybridge.

**FARNHAM - 10 TOWN AND COUNTRY RAMBLES**
Includes the Georgian town, the Craft Centre at Seale, the ruins of Waverley Abbey and two of the Hampshire villages.

**NEW TOWPATH BOOK** - for the Wey and Godalming Navigations, being a walker's guide to the 20 mile footpath. Fully revised and updated.

**ROYAL TAPESTRY** - explorers guide to West Surrey for things left by all the monarchs since 1066.

The above books are all written and illustated by Chris Howkins.

**ENJOYING WISLEY'S BIRDS** - featuring the village, the district and the garden of the Royal Horiticultural Society. A study of birdlife in West Surrey from records going back to the beginning of the century. Illustrated throughout by Chris Howkins. Researched and written by David and June Elliott.

All books published by Chris Howkins